# VIOLET BENT BACKWARDS OVER THE GRASS

*Lana Del Rey*

*Simon & Schuster*
New York   London   Toronto   Sydney   New Delhi

Dedicated to whomever's worn, warm
afternoon hands come upon these pages—
wherever you may find them—and that you
may remember that the world is conspiring
for you and to act in a manner as such.

Violet bEnt bAckwards Over The gRass

# Violet Bent Backwards Over the Grass

I went to a party
I came in hot
made decisions beforehand
my mind made up
things that would make me happy
to do them or not
each option weighed quietly
a plan for each thought

But then i walked through the door
past the open concept

and saw Violet
          bent backwards over the grass
7 years old with dandelions grasped

                    tightly in her hands
arched like a bridge in a fallen handstand
grinning wildly like a madman
with the exuberance that only doing nothing can bring
waiting for the fireworks to begin

and in that moment
i decided to do nothing about everything

forever.

Bare feet on linoleum


Stay on your path Sylvia Plath
don't fall away like all the others

Don't take all your secrets alone to your watery grave about
lovers and mother

The secrets you keep will keep you in deep like father and Amy
and brother
And all of the people you meet on the street will reiterate lies
that she uttered

Leave me in peace I cry
late at night on a slow boat bound for Catalina for no reason

tiny beads of sweat dot my forehead
could be mistaken for dewdrops if this were photo season.

But alas this is a real life - and it's been a real fight just to
keep my mind from committing treason.
Why you ask?
Because she told the townspeople I was crazy and the lies they
started to believe them

But anyway - I've moved on now

And now that I've gone scorched-earth
I'm left wondering where to go from here.
To Sonoma where the fires have just left?
South Dakota?

Would standing in front of Mount Rushmore feel like the Great
American homecoming I never had?

Would the magnitude of the scale of the sculpture take the place
of the warm embrace I've never known?

Or should I just be here now
In the kitchen
Bare feet on linoleum
Bored - but not unhappy
Cutting vegetables over boiling water that I will later turn
into stew.

What happened when I left you


Perfect petals punctuate the fabrics yellow blue
silver platters with strawberries strewn across the room

In Zimmerman with sandals on one summer dress to choose

Three girls
eyes rolled
loud laughter
dust specks lit by afternoon

My life is sweet like lemonade now there's no bitter fruit
eternal sunshine of the spotless mind
no thought of you

My thoughts have changed
my voice is higher
now i'm over u

No flickering in my head movies
projected in Bellevue

Because I captured the mood of my wish fulfilled
and sailed to Xanadu

The grief that came in waves that rolled I navigated throug

The fire from my wish as wind to a future trip to Malibu

now everything I have is perfect
nothing much to do

just perfect florals
green embroidered chairs
one dress to choose

## LA Who am I to Love You?

LA, I'm from nowhere who am I to love you
LA, I've got nothing who am I to love you

when I'm feeling this way
and I've got nothing to offer

LA
not quite the city that never sleeps
not quite the city that wakes
But the city that dreams for sure
if by dreams you mean nightmares.

LA
I'm a dreamer but
I'm from nowhere who am I to dream

LA
I'm upset!
I have complaints!
Listen to me
They say I come from money and I didn't and I didn't even ha
love and it's unfair

LA
I sold my life rights for a big check
but now I can't sleep at night and I don't know why
plus I love Saks so why did I do that when I know
it won't last

LA
I picked San Francisco because the man who doesn't love me
lives there

LA!
I'm pathetic
but so are you
can I come home now?

Daughter to no one
table for one
party of thousands of people I don't know at Delilah
where my ex-husband works
I'm so sick of this
But

Can I come home now?
Mother to no one
private jet for one
back home to the Tudor house that borne a thousand murder
plots
Hancock Park treated me very badly I'm resentful.

The witch on the corner
the neighbor nobody wanted
the reason for Garcetti's extra security.

LA!
I know I'm bad but I have nowhere else to go can I come
home now?
I never had a mother
will you let me make the sun my own now
and the ocean my son
I'm quite good at tending to things despite my upbringing
Can I raise your mountains?
I promise to keep them greener  make them my daughters
teach them about fires warn them about water

I'm lonely LA
can I come home now?

I left my city for San Francisco
I'm writing from the golden gate bridge but it's not going
as planned
I took a free ride off a billionaire and brought my
typewriter and promised myself I would stay
but
it's just not going the way I thought
it's not that I feel different
and I don't mind that it's not hot

it's just that I belong to no one, which means
there's only one place for me
the city not quite awake
the city not quite asleep
the city that's something else- something in between
the city that's still deciding
how good it should be

and also

I can't sleep without you

No one's ever really held me like you
not quite tightly
but certainly I feel your body next to me
smoking next to me
vaping lightly next to me
and I love that you love the neon lights
like me
Orange
in the distance. We both love that and I love that we have
that in common.

Also neither one of us can go back to New York.
For you, are unmoving.
As for me, it won't be my city again until I'm dead.
Fuck the New York Post!

LAAAAA!
Who am I to need you when I've needed so much
asked for so much
what i've been given I'm not yet sure I may never know that eith
until I'm dead.

For now though
what I do know  is that I don't deserve you-
not you at your best, in your splendor with towering
eucalyptus trees that sway in my dominion
Not you at your worst-
totally on fire, unlivable unbreathable.
I don't deserve you at all
You see- You have a mother
A continental shelf
a larger piece of land  from whence you came

And I am an orphan
a little seashell that rests upon your native shores
one of many that's for sure but because of that
I surely must love you closely to the most out of anyone.

For that reason-
Let me love you
don't mind my desperation
let me hold you not just for vacation but for real and forever
Make it real life, let me be a real wife to you.
Girlfriend, lover, mother, friend.
I adore you
Don't be put off by my quick-wordedness
I'm generally quite quiet, quite a meditator
actually I'll do very well down by Paramahansa Yogananda's
Realization center I'm sure.
I promise you'll barely even notice me

unless you want to notice me
unless you prefer a rambunctious child

in which case I can turn it on too!
I'm good on the stage as you may know, you may have heard of me

So either way I'll fit in just fine
so just love me by doing nothing
except for perhaps by not shaking the county line.
I'm yours if you'll have me
quietly or loudly
sincerely your daughter
regardless
you're mine.

i measure time by the days i've spent away from you

that thought occurred to me

as i watched the sky go dark from blue

# The Land of 1000 fires

Two blue steel trains run through the tunnels of your
cool blue steel eyes
Vernon
Rock quarry
The vastness of which has nothing on my beautiful mind
Dylan
i hear Dylan when i look at you
i can see it on my arm in invisible ink like a tattoo
The yin to my yang
the toughness to my unending softness
A striking example of masculinity
firm in your verticality
sure in your confrontation against all elements
and duality
The sun to my wilting daisy
The earth to the wildflower that doesn't care where it grows

Vernon
everything's burnt here
there's no escaping it
the air is fried and on fire
I've never really fallen in love
but whatever this feeling is
i wish everyone could experience it
this place feels like a person
familiar
like someone i've stood next to before
but never while i was standing next to you
Thank you
for being here
for bearing witness to my vastness

Through the years I've called you in and out of my orbit
You, in your madness
the satellite that's constellating my World
mimicking the inner chaos that i've disowned
a mirror to my past life retribution
a reflection of my sadness

If i'm going to keep on living the way that i'm living
i can't do it without you.
My feet aren't on the ground
i need your body to stand on
your name to define me
on top of being a woman
i am scared
and
ethereal
and

there are seven worlds in my eyes

i'm accessing all of them at once

one to draw my words from and my muses
another one i try and harness late at night that lies somewhe
off of the right of Jupiter
and then of course there's this one i live in
the land of 1,000 fires
that's where you come in

You
Vernon
Dylan
Two blue steel trains
running through the tunnels of your
cool blue steel eyes

to guide me far from the world of my early days
that i can't quite make out clearly
that beckon me toward high sea cliffs
on long car rides

toward a future place
a world unknown to me
made up of something surreal and dripping
Flowers in solar systems Oversized

You Vernon Dylan

no words needed to sponge up the
dark nights
no explanation for the globes in my eyes
shoulder to shoulder in the factory light
letting me be who i would have been
if everything had turned out alright

3 alternative endings
course through my blood on ice

i thrive because i say i do
and because it's what i write

But honestly if you weren't here
i don't know what things would look like

That's why no matter what world i'm in
i navigate by satellite
Vernon
Dylan
and you in your madness

two trains running
through your cool blue eyes

                    Never to Heaven


   May my eyes always stay level to the horizon
   may they never gaze as high as heaven
 to ask why
 The whys in this lifetime i've found
are inconsequential compared to the magic of the nowness
which is the solution to most questions            So as to have to ask
    May i never go where angels Fear to tread - To make the look for ans
 there are no reasons                                            in the sky
 and if there are, i'm wrong.
 But at least i won't have spent my life waiting
 looking for god in the clouds of the dawn
 listening out for otherworldly contact
 30 billion light years on

 No I'll let the others do the pondering
 and while they do i'll be on my lawn
 reading something unsubstantial with the television on

 i'll be up early to rise though of course-
 but only to make you a pot of coffee

 That's what i was thinking this morning Joe-
 that it's times like this
 as the marine layer lifts
 off the sea from the view of our favorite restaurant
 that i pray that i may always keep my eyes level to your
 eye line
 never downcast at the table cloth
 too nervous to share my innermost thoughts
 with you

 You see Joe
 it's times like this as the marine layer lifts
 off the sea on the dock where we're standing  w/ the Candle lit
 that i think to myself
 there's things you still don't know about me
 like sometimes i'm afraid my sadness is too big
 and that one day you might have to help me handle it
 but until then-

 May i always keep my eyes level to this skyline
 assessing the glittering new development
 off the coast of Long Beach
 never to heaven

 Because i have faith in man as strange as that seems
 in times like these
 and it's not just because of the warmth i've found in your
 brown eyes-
 it's because I believe in the goodness in me
 that it's firm enough to plant a flag in
 or a rosebud
 or to build a new life.

# Never to Heaven

ay my eyes always stay level to the horizon
ay they never gaze as high as heaven
o ask why
ay I never go where angels fear to tread
o as to have to ask for answers in the sky
he whys in this lifetime i've found are inconsequential
ompared to the magic of the nowness- the solution to most
uestions
here are no reasons.
nd if there are- i'm wrong
ut at least i won't have spent my life waiting
ooking for God in the clouds of the dawn
r listening out for otherworldly contact
) billion light years on
. i'll let the others do the pondering
hile i'll be sitting on the lawn
eading something unsubstantial
ith the television on
'll be up early to rise though of course-
ut only to make you a pot of coffee
hat's what i was thinking this morning Joe
hat it's times like this as the marine layer lifts
ff the sea from the view of our favorite restaurant
hat i pray that i may
lways keep my eyes level to your eyeline
ever downcast at the tablecloth
es Joe
t's times like this as the marine layer lifts
ff the sea on the dock with the candle lit
hat i think to myself
here are things you still don't know about me
ike sometimes i'm afraid my sadness is too big
nd that one day you might have to help me handle it

ut until then
ay i always keep my eyes level to this skyline
ssessing the glittering new development
ff of the coast of Long Beach
ever to heaven or revenant
Because i have faith in man as strange as that seems
n times like these
nd it's not just because of the warmth i've found in your
rown eyes
ut because i believe in the goodness in me
hat it's firm enough to plant a flag in
or a
rosebud
or to build a new life.

Tessa DiPietro

No one ever touched me without wanting to kill me
except for a healer on 6th Street and Ridgeley

Tessa DiPietro recommended casually
by a medium i no longer know

She said my number one problem was my field was untrusting
when asked what to do she paused and said
nothing
which sent me right into uncontrollable sobbing
because there's never anything you can do about the important
things

She said
Ok, one thing you can do is
picture the floor rising up to support you
and sink into the back of the bed that's behind you
too much of your energy is in front of and above you

Which for some reason made me think of a live show i had seen
Jim Morrison at the Hollywood Bowl
1968? (check date)
the blue trellised lights gave him an unusual aura
like a halo or something- made him 8 feet or taller
i remember just thinking he looked out of his body
but definitely like a God on stage

So i told her
Maybe an artist has to function a little bit above themselves
if they really want to transmit some heaven

Then she told me
Singleness of focus is the key to transmission
for an emphasis on developing inner intuition
close your eyes and feel where you hold your attention
if it's in the back of your eyes walk it down to your heart
center
and make that the new place from which your thoughts enter
clairvoyance comes mostly from this simple function

Oh- and Jim died at 27
so find another frame of reference when you're referencing
heaven
And did you ever read the lyrics to 'People Are Strange'?
He made no sense.

## Past the bushes Cypress thriving

I saw you in the mirror
you were wearing your hair differently
carrying the air differently
You say you want your hair long parted in the middle
Long in solidarity - worn for all his women

Long Beach

Aimless

your fingers wiping oil on the paper w precision
w decision like an artist never seen yet with a vision

W a reason
Stared w venom at the ceiling
not the grass
but straight ahead
Just at the skyline
w precision
laser vision

time was stopping
moving through u.
U dictated
by what moved u

  only moving never thinking

Match the sun that's slowly sinking
at the height of afternoon
In the heat of summer evening
Like a phoenix like a chemtrail like a wavelength No
one's claiming

Georgia O'Keeffe
Georgia peaches
Doing nothing but your painting
For forever
Forget teachers
Forgive him for ever leaving

love is rising
No resisting
cheeks are flushing
Now you're living

Say goodbye now
 no resisting
Live your life like
 no one's listening

Be the art that life is breathing
Be the soul the world is living.

Do what you want
For you only
Not for giving
Just for taking
No one's listening

at the end of Lime and 10th street down the road that's green
and winding
        Past the bushes cypress thriving past the chain
link fence
  and driving
            farther down the road less traveled
        there u are athleisure wear unraveled
Now I see you clear

Standing stoic blue and denim
eyes not blue but clear like
heaven

you don't want to be forgotten


You just want to disappear

SportCruiser

I took a flying lesson on my 33rd birthday instead of calling yo
or parking on the block where our old place used to be
Genesee
Genesee
Genesee
Pathetic I know, but sometimes I still like to park on that stre
and have lunch in the car just to feel close to you.
I was once in love with my life here
in that studio apartment with you
little yellow flowers on the tops of trees as our only view
out of the only window- big enough for me to see our future
through.
But it turned out I was the only one who could see it.
Stupid apartment complex. Terrible you. You who i wait for
            You

            You

            You
Like a broken record stuck on loop.

So that day on my birthday i thought something has to change,
it can't always be about waiting for u

Don't tell anyone but
part of my reasoning for taking the flight class was this idea
that if i could become my own navigator- a captain of the sky
that perhaps i could stop looking for direction- from you.

Well, what started off as an idea on a whim has turned into
something more. Too shy to explain to the owners that my first
lesson was just a one time thing. I've continued to go to classes
each week. At the precious little strip off of Santa Monica
and Bundy.
And everything was going fine we were starting with dips and
loops. And then something terrible happened-
during my fourth lesson in the sky, my instructor-
younger than i but as tough as you-  instructed me to do a
simple maneuver. It's not that i didn't do it but i was
slow to lean the SportCruiser into a right hand upward turn.
Scared. Scared that i would lose control of the plane
Not tactfully and not gently the instructor shook his head
and without looking at me said, "you don't trust yourself."
I was horrified. Feeling as though I had somehow been found out

Like he knew me- how weak i was

  Of course he was only talking about my ability as a pilot
 in the sky. But i knew it was meant for me to hear those words.
for me they held a deeper meaning.
I didn't trust myself

not just 2500 ft above the coast of Malibu
but with anything. And i didnt trust you.
I could have said something but i was quiet
because pilots aren't like poets
they don't make metaphors between life and the sky.

n the midst of this midlife meltdown navigational exercise
n self-examination, I also decided to do something else I
lways wanted to do- take sailing lessons in the vibrant bay
f Marina Del Rey. I signed up for the class as Elizabeth
rant and nobody blinked an eye. So why was I so sure that
hen I walked into the tiny shack on Bali Way someone would
ay "you're not a captain of a ship or the master of the sky"
o, the fisherman didn't care and so neither did I.
nd for a brief moment i felt more myself than ever before,
etting the self-proclaimed drunkard captain's lessons wash
ver me like the foamy tops of the sea.
idway through, my forehead burned and my hands raw from
ibing, the captain told me the most important thing i would
eed to know on the sea. Never run the ship into irons.
hat's nautical terms for not sailing the boat directly into
he wind. In order to do that though you have to know where
he wind is coming from. And you might not have time to look
o the mast or up farther to the weather vane
o you have to feel where the wind is coming from-
n your cheeks, and by the tips of the white waves-
rom which direction they're rolling.
o do this, he gave me an exercise.
e told me to close my eyes and asked me to feel on my neck
hich way the wind was blowing. I already knew I was going
o get it wrong.
The wind is coming from everywhere- I feel it all over."
 told him.
No," he said. "The wind is coming from the left. The port side."
 sat waiting for him to tell me, "you don't trust yourself."
ut he didn't, so I said it for him.
I don't trust myself."
e laughed, gentler than the pilot but still not realizing
hat my failure in the exercise was hitting me at a much
eeper level.
It's not that you don't trust yourself," he said. "It's simply
hat you're not a captain. It isn't what you do."
hen he told me he wanted me to practice every day so I would
et better.
Which grocery store do you go to?" he asked
To the Ralphs in the Palisades," I replied.
Ok. When you're in the Ralphs in the Palisades - I want you-
s you're walking from your car to the store - to close your
yes and feel which way the wind is blowing. Now I don't
ant you to look like a crazy person crouching in the middle
f the parking lot but everywhere you go- I want you to
ry and find which way the wind is coming in from and then determine
 if it's from the port or starboard side so when you're
ack on the boat you'll have a better sense of it."
 thought his advice was adorable. I could already picture
yself in the parking lot squinting my eyes with perfect
ousewives looking on. I could picture myself growing a
etter sense of which way the wind was blowing and as I did
 tiny bit of deeper trust also began to grow within myself.

I thought of mentioning it but I didn't.
Because captains aren't like poets
they don't make metaphors between the sea and sky.
And as I thought that to myself
I realized-
that's why I write.

All of this circumnavigating the earth
was to get back to my life
6 trips to the moon for my poetry to arise
I'm not a captain
I'm not a pilot
I write
I write.

Quiet Waiter- Blue forever

  You move like water sweet baby sweet waiter
making the night smile to no one you xcater
quiet wood worker from midnight till later
my lover my laughter my armor my maker
The way that I feel with you is something like aching
inside my stomach the cosmos are baking
A universe hung like a mobile
the alignment of these planets unique
In me the earth moves around the sun
no land all sea

water world
sun chaser
tropic of cancer
southern equater
i'm the crying crustacean
sunbathing on paper
moon.
Let's rewrite the beginning of this primordial ooze
shall we my love?
Am i being brazen for saying this year makes me feel
like we could've wrote it better
than him (rhyme w moon?)
But who am I          dreaming on paper
just a girl in love scribbling in journals
rearranging the salt and pepper
                        the
in love with you
my ~~blue~~ quiet waiter
~~forever~~
summer
~~quiet waiter~~
weather Blue forever ?
Call me when you're done with work/ the darker the better
i'll pick you up later

the darker the Bon

Altering)

In love w/ you

my Blue forever

Summer quiet waiter

call me when youre done w/ work

the Later the Better

the Later the Better?

Call me when youre done w/ work
the later the better    ?
the later the better

IN
M

Su
Bl

Call me
WITH wor
I'll PICK UP
the darker the Bett

## Quiet Waiter Blue Forever

You move like water sweet baby sweet waiter
making the night smile to no one you cater
silent woodworker from midnight till later
my lover my laughter my armor my maker
The way that i feel with you is something like aching
inside of my stomach the cosmos are baking
a universe hung like a mobile
the alignment of these planets unique
in me the earth moves around the sun
no land all sea
water world
sun chaser
tropic of cancer
southern equator
i'm the crying crustacean
sunbathing on paper
moon.
Let's rewrite the beginning of this primordial ooze
shall we my love
Am i being brazen for saying this year makes me feel
like we could've written it better
than him?
But who am i
just a girl in love dreaming on paper
rearranging the salt for the pepper
in love with you
my quiet waiter
Summer
blue
Forever
call me when you're done with work
i'll pick you up later
the darker the better
five after midnight
the darker the better

My bedroom is a sacred place now - There are children
           at the foot of my bed

Last year when I wrote you my last letter
(the beginning of my future poetry)
I acknowledged who you were for the first time.
I didn't call you by any other name
I let you know that I knew the true nature of your heart-
that it was evil
that it convinced me that darkness is real
that the devil is a real devil
and that monsters don't always know they are monsters.

But projection is an interesting thing
after you burned the house down
you tried to convince me that i was the one holding the
matches
You told me that I din't know what I had done
You said I don't know who I am

But I do know who I am.

I love Rose Gardens
I buy violets every time someone leaves me
I love the great sequoias of Yosemite
and if you asked my sister to describe the first thing she
thinks of when she thinks of me
she would say
woodsmoke

I'm gentle
I'm funny
when I'm drunk
though I haven't been drunk for 14 years

I go on trips to the beach with my friends who don't know
that I'm crazy.
I can do that.
I can do anything-
even leave you

because my bedroom is a sacred place now
there are children at the foot of my bed
telling me stories about the friends they pretend to hate
that they will make up with tomorrow-
and there are fresh cut flowers that i grew myself
in vases on nightstands hand-carved by old pals from Big Sur
and the longer i stay here, the more i am sure
that the more i step into becoming a poet the less
  i will fall into being with you
the more i step into my poetry the less i will fall into
being with you
            the more i step into
                    my poetry the less i will
all into being with you
        the more i step into my poetry the less i will
  fall into being
                    with you
the
    more
          i step into becoming a poet
the less i will fall into
bed
with
    you.

## In the hills of Benedict Canyon

Love has room to grow in the hills of Benedict Canyon
My green typewriter light is on
and two months' time between me and my last man
No double murder plots looming over neighbors' vacant lots
that i look upon at twilight, still light enough for the
Starline bus to be carrying on. I listen to the hippie
spouting nonsense at the  foot of Bella Drive
hammering on about Sharon and the sanctity of life
I listen on intently
thanks for the free ride
and for reminding me that everything comes down to a story
and to laugh when you could cry.

But finally I have no reason for tears
not tonight at 7:27
first time in months i feel close to heaven
in the hills of Benedict Canyon
the background hum of the television
love has room to grow.
No more secrets no more reasons to put off what I already know
No more big projects
no new dev breaking ground on Sunset
no big builds lasting too long up on Mulholland
no joint ventures  fracturing.
no unchained  melodies enchanting the  bars in my head.

No. Just no news, nothing going on at 7:27
not quite ready for dinner
the background hum of television

Me- standing out on the deck
wondering what phase of twilight the sky is in
and contemplating how the Dodgers are doing
and reaching for the  phone
to call an old friend.

You're only as happy as your least happy child

                              happy


you thought i was rich and i am but not how you think
i live in a Tudor house under the freeway in Mar Vista
by the beach
when you call i take my phone outside to the picnic table
that i bought from the Rose Bowl
and i listen to the rushing cars above
and think about the last time you visited me
the last time we made love
how the noise got louder and louder during rush hour
until it sounded like the sea
and it felt like the ocean was the sky
and that i was flying because you were two feet taller than m
until you took me in your arms
and i could touch the stars
and they all fell down around my head
and i became an angel
and you put me to bed

happy

People think that i'm rich and i am but not how they think
i have a truck with a gold key chain in the ignition
and on the back it says: happy joyous and free

happy

and when i drive
i think about the last time my friends were driving with me
how the radio was so loud that we couldn't hear the words
so we became the music

happy

They write that i'm rich and i am but not how they think
i have a safe i call the boyfriend box
and in it every saved receipt
every movie theater ticket just to remind me
of all the things i've loved and lost and loved again
unconditionally

You joke that i'm rich and i am but not how you think
i live in a Tudor house under the freeway
off of Rose Avenue 12 blocks from the beach
and when you call i put your sweater on
and put you on speaker
and chat for hours underneath the trees
and think about the last time you were here lying next to me
how the noise from the cars got louder and louder
during rush hour
until it sounded like a river or a stream
and it felt like we were swimming
but it wasn't just a dream
we were just

happy

## Sugarfish

Lemme stick to something sweet
sugar on my hands and feet
Sugarfish San Vicente
sugar sugar in my teeth
from your kiss you texting me
from the movie theater seat
Dodger Stadium Slurpee
white confection in the sea
powder waves froth over me
A fortune teller once told me
do things that you think are sweet and a sweet man is sure t
follow.

So I made a bath that night of honey
dipped my toes in rose and money
stayed all night in that bathwater
even some I swallowed.

Now there's so much sugar on me
I can't keep the bees off of me
even most of my thoughts are charming
some are blue and borrowed

Sugar sugar lips and teeth
fingertips touch emojis
hard forever
hearts on fleek
bb please come over

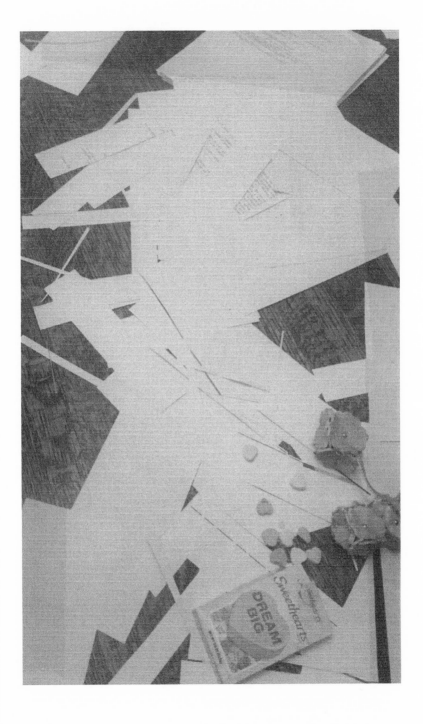

## ringtone

I put my third phone in the waistband of my leggings
only u have this number
6 plus vibrates with your own ringtone
i smile when i hear simulated children laughing
cause i know it's u
it's the little things that make me smile
i keep them just for myself
i like u so much
but it makes me nervous when u don't call
under my breath i say
Don't make me be resilient
i so want to be soft
if u let me be myself
u will be the first one who ever did.

                    In the flats of Melrose


What will it take for me not to feel like the train will
run away with me bound up like the sad heroine tied to the las
car
What will it take for me not to need you
so I can just have you for fun
and for who you really are

Not you as the savior
not me as Ophelia
not us putting our faith in the public's dark art

Topanga on Sunday?
two cats in the yard
NPR rumbling quietly
a fire in the hearth
me with a knowingness deep in my heart
that nothing could stop me no valley too far
to walk through in darkness to keep us apart.

And that we don't need fighting to find resolution
that not every marriage ends in the dissolution

that I don't need you
but I want you
because you're so cool
and I'm not that damaged
and ur not hell-bent on being some indie director
or whatever pipe dream you and your friends are smoking
That it's enough just for us
to be sitting in the flats of Melrose
my heart on fire
a tallboy cracked open
 I love you Josiah
 I'm sorry I'm still broken
but I could still make you happy.
Let's pour one out
 to knowing
 not hoping

Thanks to the Locals

I ran away from you to Lake Arrowhead
I didn't tell you where I was going
I knew I had a 24 hour grace period before you were done makin
your film
I went to an aa meeting
And my share read like a tale of a battered housewife

I felt everyone's eyes on me
The rehab kids in the back row stopped throwing spitballs at
each other and stared at me
I fucking hate my life.

I waited after the meeting in the parking lot for any of the
local ladies
to come up to me
Only one did, Kira.
"I don't really have much advice for you" she said

I was in over my head
out of my league
In the wrong place wrong season wrong time wrong face
and I knew it
But I didn't know what to do

You asked me to marry you
You said your mother was dying and you couldn't fathom your
life without a woman in it.

I was tempted but it didn't seem like a good enough offer
I wanted more than that
even though I've never had anything.
Not one person to call if I changed my dollar in for quarters t
ask what they thought about it.

But there's always been just a little tiny piece of me inside
the size of a small slice of angel cake that knew
somewhere somehow
That I deserved better than someone like you.

So I got back into my truck in the dark
my little yellow pamphlet with two numbers on it that I would
never call crumpled up
Kira with her local area code and gratefully also her

ponsor, Gail from Palmdale.

didn't feel better and I didn't use the numbers but I thought
hat I had been very brave that I did the best I could, sharing
n a big room, tears streaming down my face in my high school
lannel
ust to say

The man that I love hates me.
ut it would be easier to stay."

s the last person's lights flooded over my windshield
he night became very quiet
nd i thought-

f I go back and I end it
ow would I handle driving down your street and it becoming a
istant memory
ot reality
o longer sweet.
weet the way it tastes in my mouth to say your name
weet like when I was young, driving down those roads before we
ere done
efore any big battles were lost or won
nbeknownst to everyone
xcept for you and me.

s Sweet as a junkie's limited concept of love can be.
thought cause u were clean u were a lot like me
anting to be closer to something big and free.
ut some people need their secrets

nd now my greatest battle will be
his unchained melody
n my heart
rom not having you next to me.
o shut the door on the past and step
lindly
nto the abyss
o destination intact
he only direction set in the Compass -  to move forward.

o I drove
ack and forth
n the Rim of the World Hwy
nd the beauty of its name reminded me

That I was beautiful
That some things are beautiful for no reason.
Not everyone needs to pretend to love their girlfriend just
because their mother is dying
or because they're afraid of a change in season...

Anyway
I don't have a pretty couplet to give resolution to this poem
nothing very eloquent to say

except that I was brave
and it would've been easier to stay

I'm writing my future

The universe exists
        because we are aware of it

Paradise is Very Fragile


Paradise is very fragile
and it seems like it's only getting worse
down here in Florida we are fighting toxic red tides.
Massive fish kills
Not to mention hurricanes and rising sea levels
Back in Los Angeles things aren't looking much better
my tree house that had been standing for 60 years succumbed to
the Woolsey fires
who would've thought this year at 33 you would be taken out
from under me
after all those years
built from the ground up by hand by your very first owner.
Quiet World War 1 aviation pilot
I tried to save you
but the horses and german shepherds were more important


Paradise is very fragile and it seems that it's only
getting worse
Our leader is a megalomaniac and we've seen that before
but never because it was what the country deserved.
My friends tell me to stop calling 911 on the culture
but it's either that or I 5150 myself.
They don't understand
I'm a dreamer
And I had big dreams for the country
Not for what it could do but for how it could feel
How it could think how it could dream.
I know I know -who am I to dream for you
it's just that in my own mind I was born with a little bit of
paradise. I was lucky in that way
not like my husband- who was born and raised in hell.
I always had something gentle to give-
all of me in fact
it's one of the beautiful things about me
it's one of the beautiful things about nature
But lately I've been thinking that I wish someone had told me
when I was younger more about the inhabitants that thrive off
of paradise. That should they take too much there will be
nothing left to give.
Not everyone's nature is good or golden

and you can't fight what's in your nature.

that's all I kept thinking as we were fighting the fires
in Agoura
that I'm tired of fighting you.
Tired of you taking from me

Paradise is very fragile and it's only getting worse
and every time you leave I seem to think about the curse
bestowed upon Eve
that faithful eve
she took that bite
from that fruitful tree
You breathe me in
kundalini
in this summer night
you in front of me
And you take and you take and you take and you take
but you taste like the beach in a kiss
candy for my watery eyes
in my veins that roll you run citrus
watercolor images of serpents on orange trees quietly arise
and grow sweet in my midst
And I keep thinking I could do this forever
just like this
but my heart is very fragile
and I have nothing left to give

                    Salamander

et out of my blood salamander
  can't seem to blow off enough steam to get you out of my head
oulCycle you to death
un you out of my blood to San Pedro
nd yet everywhere I go it seems there you are.
nd there I am.

  don't want to sell my stories anymore stop pushing me.
  want to leave them underneath the nightstand to be forgotten
r remembered should my thoughts come upon them in the middle
f the night after a beach day
r by you some afternoon-
o thumb through- with your worn warm after-work hands.


 love u
ut you don't understand me

ou see I'm a real poet

ly life is my poetry
ny lovemaking is my legacy

ly thoughts are not for sale
hey're about nothing
nd beautiful and for free

 wish you could get that
nd love that about me

ecause things that can't be bought can't be evaluated
nd that makes them beyond human reach.

ntouchable
afe
therworldly

nable to be deciphered or metabolized
omething metaphysical

ike a view of the sea
n a summer day on the most perfect winding road
aken in from your car seat window

A thing perfect and ready to become a part of the texture o
the fabric of Something more ethereal
like Mount Olympus
where Zeus and Athena and the rest of the immortals play

I love u
But u don't understand me

You see
I'm a real poet

My life is my poetry
My lovemaking is my legacy

You can have a life beyond your wildest dreams

all you have to do is change everything...

all you have to do is change everything
All you have to do is change everything
all you have to do is change everything

Haikus

Jasmine in the air
the burden of fame is real
never felt so clear

You in the soft light
the 405 from Venice
a river of red

Wondering if it's
astronomical twilight
or civil twilight

Every night I die
when I give myself to you
sad but beautiful

Poets- like comics
are inherently quite sad
better off alone

I stepped on a bird
cried in my new boyfriend's arms
to live is to kill

For years I begged you
to just take me in your arms
you wouldn't. Couldn't.

Babe let's go to town
buy something sweet - pink grapefruit
eat it with sugar

No big decisions
to the lake or to the sea
My only question

Open the front door
hello I say to no one
I know no one's home

notes for a poet

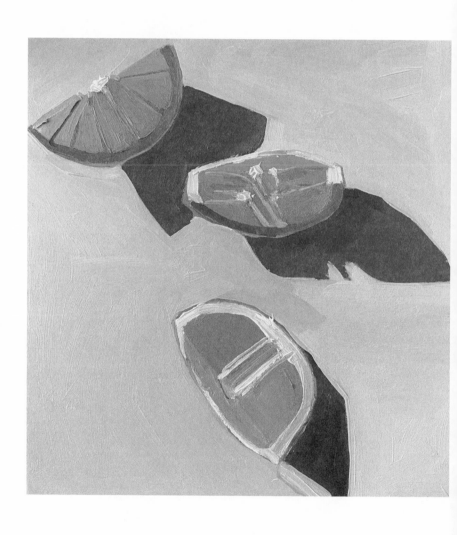

Simon & Schuster
1230 Avenue of the Americas
New York, NY 10020

First Simon & Schuster hardcover edition September 2020

SIMON & SCHUSTER and colophon are registered trademarks
of Simon & Schuster, Inc.

For information about special discounts for bulk purchases,
please contact Simon & Schuster Special Sales at 1-866-506-1949
or business@simonandschuster.com.

The Simon & Schuster Speakers Bureau can bring authors
to your live event. For more information or to book an event,
contact the Simon & Schuster Speakers Bureau at 1-866-248-3049
or visit our website at www.simonspeakers.com.

Manufactured in the United States of America

10  9  8  7  6  5  4  3  2  1

Library of Congress Control Number: 2020942127

ISBN 978-1-9821-6728-8
ISBN 978-1-9821-6730-1 (ebook)